©Josh "Atlas" Aultman 2021

The Fox in the Box

This is a story of a fox who was once stuck in a
box.

He asked his neighbor, the Ox
'Have you seen my socks?

His friendly neighbor said "They are in the **box**."

After looking in the biggest **box,**

7

He fell in and couldn't see the top
Everything went dark

Stuck in the box,
He was still smart as a fox

So – He studied the **box**
He studied from the bottom to the top

He looked at the **box** wall, it was very tall
He thought "if I climb this tall wall it would make for a bad fall"

So, noticing some grass — He tried to dig
He thought "hey, I'm not too big"

His paws dug like quick, felt like they were on fire
He dug and dug, until he was tired

As the fox laid on the **box** floor
He realized there was a **box** door

He thought, this **box** must belong to the boxing ox

16

Then in a flash, two pairs of socks fell down from the **box** top

17

The ox peered in and said "good thing you looked around."

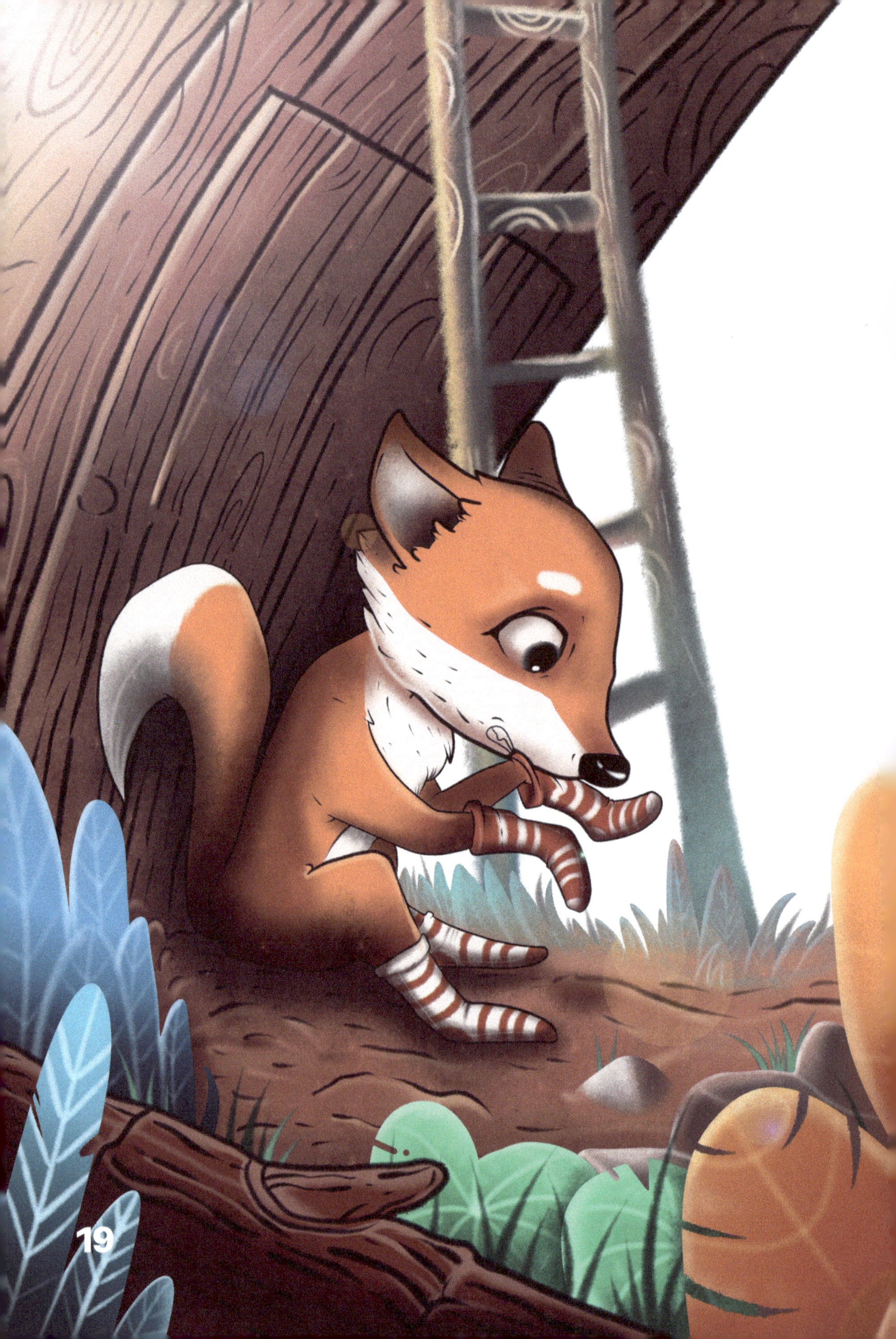

The fox replied, "you got that right" as he thought "shew, I'm done with this fight"
And
grabbed his socks

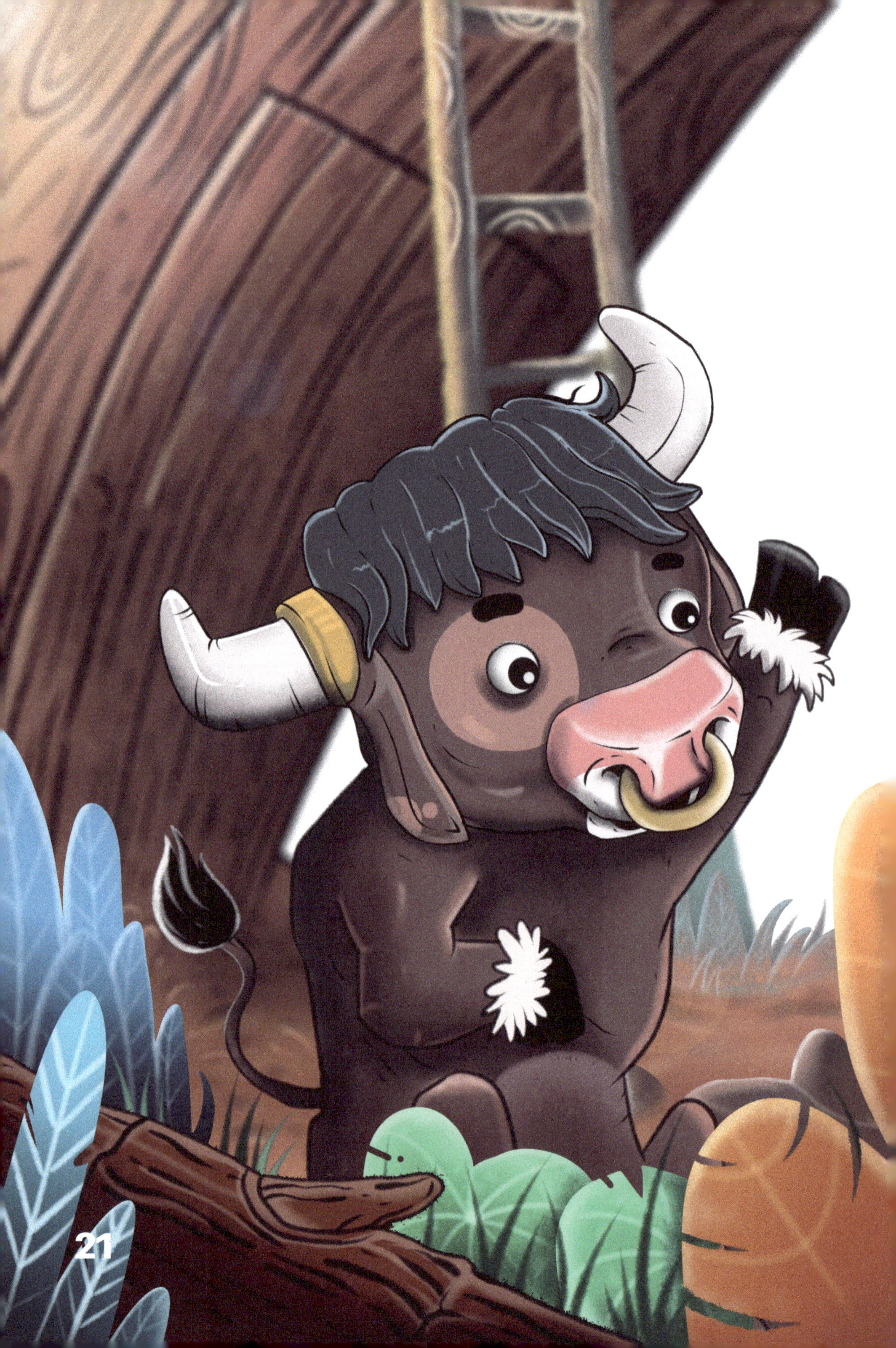

Then all in a flash, he looked back at the ox

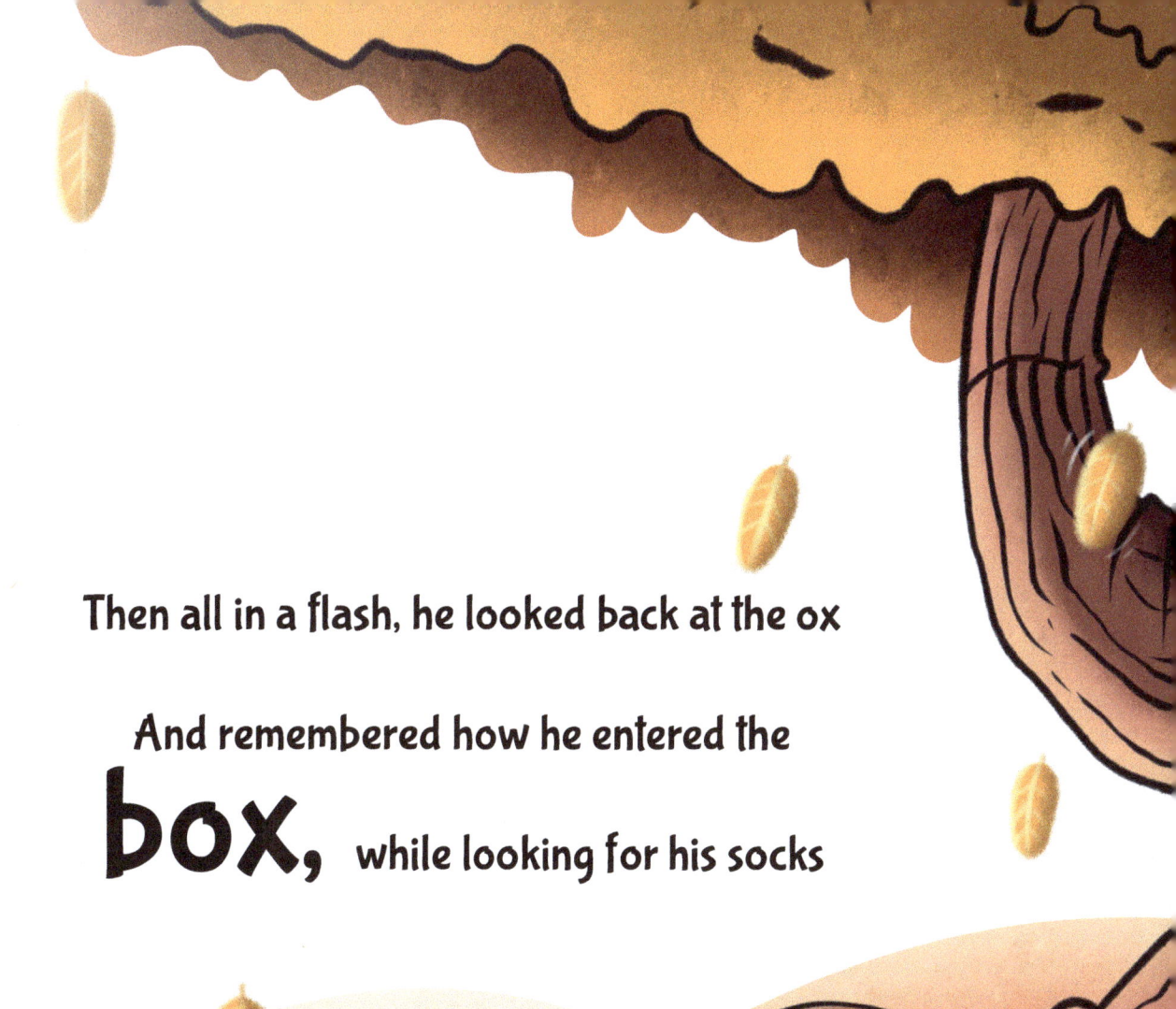

And remembered how he entered the
box, while looking for his socks

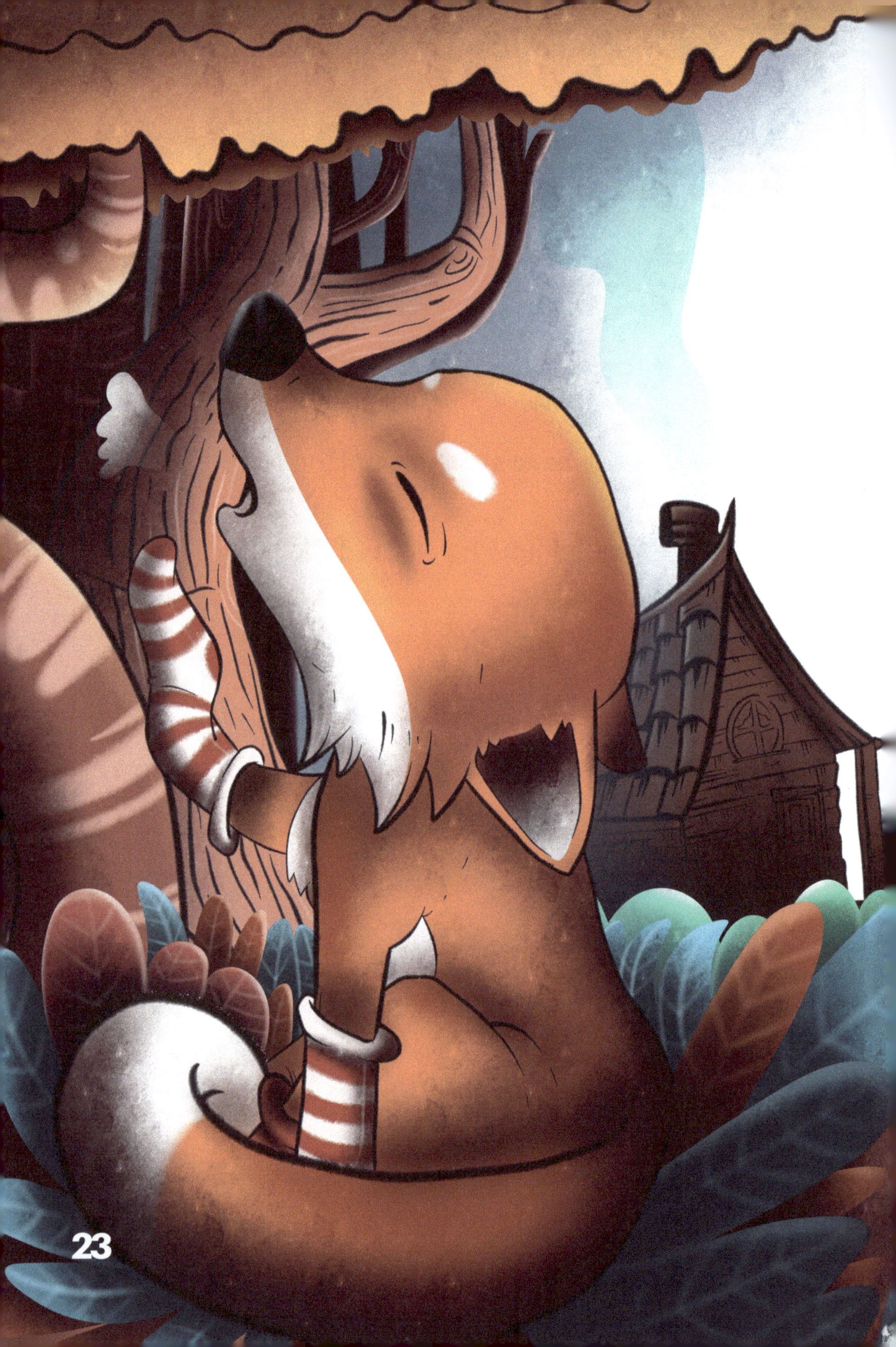

Then he left his box with his socks and became a sleepy fox

And with his socks on tight, he was ready to sleep through a cold night

26

He dreamed like foxes dream, and in the morning he put on new socks

He was ready to join his box-fighting team.

28

The End

Leadership Principles

1. How important do you think teamwork was to finding the fox's socks?

2. How important do you think organization is to the fox?

3. Do you think teamwork was used in this story?

Looking for more?
Go to
www.leaders-KIT.com